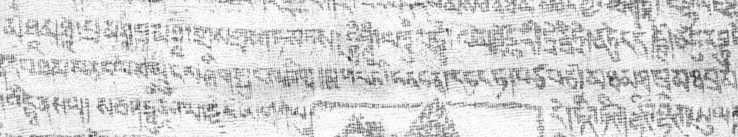

People within a Landscape

A collection of images of Nepal

photography and text
Bert Willison — Shirley Bourke

Published by
THE MOUNTAINEERS
SEATTLE
with
THE FOUR SHERPA TRUST
NEW PLYMOUTH/NEW ZEALAND

Mt Dhaulagiri (8172m) from above Kagbeni (looking south).

''There's only one escape from crowds Live in the sky
among the clouds.''

Lama Proverb

Foreword

The Kingdom of Nepal holds an ongoing fascination for the rest of the world.

Those who visit its mountains and valleys, its ancient cities and villages, tend to carry with them forever a longing to return. This book recognises that longing with images of the country and its people in many moods.

One of the great reasons for the huge growth of adventure travel in Nepal is the quality of the Nepalese people, particularly the Sherpas, who serve mountaineering and trekking expeditions with cheerful comradeship and willing, but never servile, assistance.

The aim of this book — to contribute help for families of Nepalese hill people who lose their lives or are injured during these expeditions is a noble one. The education of their children is very close to my heart.

Ed Hillary

Mt Everest (8848m), Sagarmatha, upper left, viewed from the vicinity of Syangboche. The impressive ridge partially obscuring Everest is Nuptse-Lhotse.

*"God will be pleased if people
keep things beautiful."*

The High Lama of Thyangboche Monastery.

The "Fishtail", Machapuchare (6993m) and Annapurna II
(7937m) seen from a hilltop near the Deorali Pass. A
prayer flag in the foreground catches the breeze to send
its message across the world.

This woman's ear and nose ornaments are typical of Nepal
and her necklace of coral has religious significance as well
as displaying her wealth.

"...One of the ways to better understanding may lie up ridges, along mountain tracks, and through quiet forests, where minds can rest and prepare for action again."

Rewi Alley

Langtang massif shows through the trees above Lama Hotel in the Langtang Valley.

Rhododendron barbatum, Langtang Valley.

"The Himalayas have a way of getting into your blood. The fascinating people and places we had seen haunted our dreams and wove a magic spell through our waking moments."

Journey to Little Tibet
National Geographic Society.

A typical Buddhist painting of "WHITE TARA" who represents the fertile aspect of compassion. White Tara may be easily recognised by her seven eyes. She is said to have been born from a tear of compassion which fell from the eye of Avalokiteshvara.

Chortens, small pagoda-like holy memorials, are here set in a mani or prayer-stone wall. These were photographed near Muktinath, upper Kali Gandaki Valley, after a snowfall.

Contents

Introduction

"As I stepped out on my first day's march in the Himalayas
a strange exhilaration thrilled me. I kept squeezing my fists
together and saying emphatically to myself and to the
universe at large: Oh yes! Oh yes! This really is splendid!
How splendid! How splendid!"

Sir Francis Younghusband 1924

The same sentiments kept coming through when I first considered going trekking, as the phrase "trekking is addictive" seemed to crop up regularly in reading material. Now, after eight visits to the Himalaya I have the urge to show it's magic to those who have not experienced it, and recall it to those who have.

This book aims to portray the unique mixture of people, cultures, religions and mountains that are Nepal. The material used is a selection of images taken over a period of thirteen years.

In October 1985, while trekking in the Annapurna area, my party was trapped for ten days high above Tilicho Lake by unseasonable heavy snowfalls. Four of our Sherpas were killed by an avalanche while attempting to force a route out from our campsite.

The funds earned by this book will be devoted to continuing the work of the Four Sherpa Trust set up by members of the trapped party to honour the memory of these fine young men.

Sherpas act as guides, porters, cooks, interpreters and companions, and one of the essential ingredients of any trekking trip to Nepal is close and rewarding contact with them.

It has always saddened me that so many Sherpas lose their lives while assisting climbing expeditions and guiding trekking parties. It is my hope that now, in some small way, I can help to improve the lives of the wives and children left behind, and the men who are injured and unable to work.

"People and mountains belong to each other
and are inseparable."

Colin Turnbull

Each time, as the plane clears the foothills and comes in to land at Kathmandu Airport, I get a strange feeling in the pit of my stomach. Perhaps it is the sight of the neat houses and cultivated terraces which brings this sensation, or the memory of past experiences that flash into my mind at the sight of the mountains stretching away into the distance on both sides of the aircraft as we begin our descent.

Whichever it is, I know I have finally arrived when I enter the airport building — there is only one Kathmandu Airport.

As long as that sensation keeps coming I shall keep returning to this poor but richly endowed country that is Nepal.

I close this introduction as it began, with a quotation from Sir Francis Younghusband:-

"The more you see of the Himalayas
the more you want to see."

Bert Willison

Trekkers on the trail above Thyangboche
Monastery. Ama Dablam (6856m) dominates the
scene.

History of Trekking and Adventure Tourism

Adventure tourism in the Himalayas began in 1964 with the registration in Nepal of the first trekking company in the world, Mountain Travel.

Its founder, Colonel Jimmy (J. O. M.) Roberts, ex-British Army in India, tells of how he made lists of what would be needed to start − eight sleeping pads, eight this, eight that. He remembers writing down eight tents (eight he thought might be a reasonable sized party to handle) then scratching it out and writing "four". "Let 'em share", he thought.

A small advertisement was placed in a holiday magazine, and his first clients came to do an Everest trek in the early spring of 1965. A story circulating a year or so later said that first party was a trio of American grandmothers, and that "Roberts was horrified at what he had taken on".

Roberts says in fact, that two of them were unmarried so were unlikely to have been grandmothers, and a more sporting trio of enthusiastic and appreciative ladies he has never since handled.

He used Sherpas as trek staff because an experienced pool of sirdars, cooks and porters with whom he was familiar was already in existence from his and other mountaineering expeditions. The following year, when Mountain Travel was beginning to give Sherpas a fair amount of employment, coincided with the end of mountaineering activity for three years.

Khumbu, the Sherpa tribal homeland near Mount Everest was already suffering from the economic effects of the almost complete closure of once profitable trade with Tibet due to Chinese influence, so the new source of employment was a godsend. It gave them not charity but money and self-respect, says Roberts.

Nowadays many different races are employed in trekking throughout the Himalayas by a multitude of companies, but Roberts maintains that the trekking companies of Nepal have an unfair advantage over those in other parts of Central Asia by the use of Sherpas who "repay their wages many times over with willing work, loyalty and comradeship. . .serving superbly without trace of servility".

Sherpas are a tribe of Tibetan extraction from a particular area, but the name has come to be applied to anyone climbing or trekking as a guide − a sort of accolade for hardy dependability in the mountains.

The idea of adventure trekking caught on, and only a year after its start, Colonel Roberts had to start considering the problem of "how big?" if the quality of trekkers' mountain experience was not to be impaired. He wondered whether he should turn people away, but realised that would not reduce the numbers of people coming to trek. Other companies were beginning to enter the field so it seemed better to expand and try to set a standard to ensure that the good name created for trekking in Nepal did not suffer.

The growth of wilderness travel in the last few years has been phenomenal, and tourism is now Nepal's largest foreign exchange earner by far. Registered trekking companies pay tax on their profits which benefit the Nepalese economy, plus earnings in the form of Sherpas' and porters' wages and food purchases for trek parties reach people in remote mountain areas.

Guided wilderness travel has meant that people from all over the world who never dreamed it would be possible, have been able to enjoy an expeditionary type holiday in the Himalayas.

But words of warning from Colonel Roberts in 1988 could be echoed by others. In 1987 more than 20,000 people visited the Annapurna area alone. Trails became overcrowded and dirty, and the majority of trekkers were travelling independently, living cheaply in tea houses many of which were ill-equipped for the numbers.

"The here today, gone tomorrow trekker lowers the quality of the experience for all who pass that way and this, together with the reputation spread, can keep others from coming later who might travel with a well-run agency", he said. He saw an urgent need for some sort of control despite an official drive to increase overall tourist numbers.

Today, trekking is only a part of the adventure tourism network which has been built up.

In Nepal it goes from the lowland jungles of Chitwan and Bandhavgarh National Parks with the comfortable jungle lodges and tented camps of Tiger Tops which pioneered this sort of trip, through wildlife safaris, special interest treks, white water rafting "treks" on Nepal's rushing rivers, to treks of varying length and difficulty from the lowlands to the foohills and on to the highest mountains.

High above the Kali Gandaki a Sherpa returns from an unsuccessful attempt to visit the Dhaulagiri Icefall due to deep snow. However the snow has other compensations of a photographic nature. The Nilgiris are the peaks across the valley.

Roberts Story

*"For long miles into the heart of morning, Miles
and miles, far over land and sea, Past enchanted
regions of forewarning, Dawns at last the land
that dims all these."*

Roberts

Colonel Jimmy (J. O. M.) Roberts, who introduced to the world the concept of commercially arranged walking holidays in Nepal, joined the old British Army in 1936, an 18 year old fresh from English public school.

He claims to have chosen that career because he was "unqualified for any more intellectual employment", but above all, because he wanted a lifetime of climbing in the Himalayas. An appointment in 1937 to a Ghurka regiment with headquarters at Dharamsala, 1835m (6000ft) up on the flanks of the Dhauladar Range in what is now the north Indian state of Himachal Pradesh, not only gave him a head start to achieving his ambition, but also laid the foundation for a lifetime's appreciation and love for the peoples of Nepal.

Up to three months local leave could be granted to British officers in India annually, and leave applications for adventurous shooting or climbing trips in the passes of Central Asia were sure to be granted.

The whole of the Karakorums and Himalayas, except for Nepal, were open to climbers then, with little need for permits. Visits to Kathmandu however were by invitation only, and the rest of the country remained totally closed to foreigners until 1948.

Climbing extensively in other areas but always dreaming of Nepal, Jimmy Roberts had to wait for 14 years before he could visit that country. He has never lost a sense of privilege in being there, although he has now lived in Nepal for more than 30 years.

After distinguished service in North Burma during the second world war, a daring, almost successful attempt on Kanchenjunga and several more mountaineering expeditions, in 1950 he joined the first climbing expedition to the Annapurna region. At the end of this trip he walked across to Pokhara with one Sherpa and found his private Mecca.

He still believes there is no other mountain view in the world to equal Machapuchare and Annapurna, "Hanging in the sky above the green Pokhara plain".

In 1958 he was dealt an ace with an appointment as military attache at the British Embassy in Kathmandu. When he retired from the army at the end of this three-year appointment he decided to stay in Nepal and create his own means of employment there.

Remembering the agents in pre-war Kashmir who provided camp gear, staff, porters and food for climbing parties at an agreed rate and the lessons learned during many years of expeditionary mountaineering, the idea of a trekking agency was born.

His company, Mountain Travel, the first of its kind and with staff specially trained to handle clients unused to Nepal conditions, was registered in 1964.

His philosophy of trekking formulated then — "to show the mountains, valleys, villages and people of Nepal . . . to enjoy to the full without organisational worries or distractions" is still carried out by the company, since 1974 incorporated as the trekking arm of Tiger Tops Mountain Travel International.

Colonel Jimmy Roberts is a consulting director and still plays a large part in choosing and training of trek staff.

Colonel Jimmy (J.O.M.) Roberts (*left*) outside his Pokhara home. A woman relaxes at a 'people place' on a trail north of Pokhara (*above*).

TIBET

NEPAL

SAIPAL
7050

KANJIROBA
6883

DHAULAGIRI
8172

JOMOSON ●

ANNAPURNA I
8091

MANASL
8156

MACHAPUCHARE
6993

ANNAPURNA II
7937

BENI ●

HIMALCHU
7893

POKHARA ●

GOR ●

MUGL

NEPALGANJ ●

BUTWAL ●

INDIA

ROYAL CHI
NATIONAL

BHAIRAHAWA ●

"A CAUTIONARY TALE"
The spelling of various place names,
mountains and rivers is subject to
considerable variation even in
authoritative publications so readers are
asked to be aware of this while reading
this book. The same problem occurs
with the heights of mountains.

Due to their altitude the Himalayas have a marked effect on the climate of Nepal and Tibet, in fact they act to entirely separate two different climatic zones.

The section shows how the foothills and later the Himalayas themselves cause precipitation to fall on the southern slopes and why the Tibetan plateau, and to a lesser degree the mid valleys, are so arid. This is especially the case during the monsoon (late May to September).

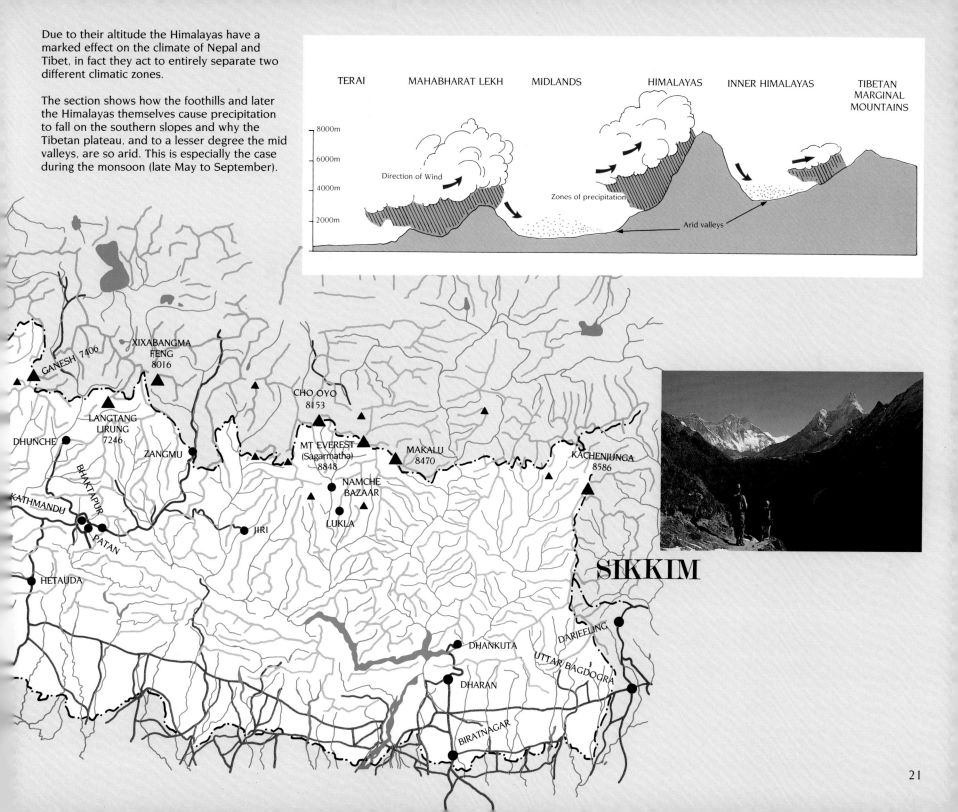

TERAI   MAHABHARAT LEKH   MIDLANDS   HIMALAYAS   INNER HIMALAYAS   TIBETAN MARGINAL MOUNTAINS

8000m
6000m
4000m
2000m

Direction of Wind

Zones of precipitation

Arid valleys

GANESH 7406

XIXABANGMA FENG 8016

CHO OYO 8153

LANGTANG LIRUNG 7246

DHUNCHE

ZANGMU

MT EVEREST (Sagarmatha) 8848

MAKALU 8470

KACHENJUNGA 8586

BHAKTAPUR

KATHMANDU

PATAN

NAMCHE BAZAAR

LUKLA

JIRI

HETAUDA

SIKKIM

DHANKUTA

DARJEELING

UTTAR BAGDOGRA

DHARAN

BIRATNAGAR

Tropical Jungle to the High Mountains

The pictures in this book have been chosen to illustrate the transition from the Terai, which is an extension into Nepal of the plains of India, to the point where trekking gives way to mountaineering. We will begin our journey with a visit to Tiger Tops in the jungle of the Royal Chitwan National Park and then progress up through the lower valleys and ridges with their tropical character and bananas, sugar cane and other luxuriant plant growth. When we reach the middle valleys the people will come from a different ethnic or tribal background, the architecture of the villages will have gone through several different styles, the plants and trees will show adaptations to the higher altitude and cooler climate. The transition continues as the higher valleys and villages are reached. Ultimately the trees give way to sparse vegetation and later, as with the upper Kali Gandaki, to the mountainous desert of the Tibetan plateau beyond the reach of the monsoon rains. The major unifying force in the journey is, apart from the people and the landscape which are constantly changing, the mountains. Add all these factors and the result is what makes the Nepal experience unique.

"None of the books or photographs studied before leaving home had even slightly prepared me for such majesty. Truly this is something that does have to be seen to be believed, and that once seen must be continually yearned for when left behind, becoming as incurable a fever of the spirit as malaria is of the body."

Dervla Murphy 1967

North from Royal Chitwan National Park the mountains of the Nepal Himalaya rise above the jungle and foothills, *left*. Built in sal (Shorea robusta) forest on the banks of the Reu River, only 150m above sea level, Tiger Tops Lodge *right*, is the starting point for a variety of wildlife adventures.

(Photos on this page by courtesy TIGER TOPS)

Royal Chitwan National Park

The park, officially gazetted in 1973, lies approximately one hundred and twenty kilometres south-west of Kathmandu and covers an area of 932 square kilometres. Originally established in 1962 by the late King Mahendra as a rhinoceros preserve to protect the rare one-horned rhinoceros from extinction, the park contains a wide variety of animals, birds, reptiles and fish as well as suitable forest, grassland and riverine habitats.

Bengal tiger (Panthera tigris) seen here resting in the shade. (Photo: Tiger Tops)

Evening calm. The Narayani River, Royal Chitwan National Park, photographed during a visit to Tiger Tops Tented Camp.

Left. Elephant grass is aptly named. In this picture a group from Tiger Tops is searching for animals, mainly rhinoceros, deer, monkeys and if very lucky, tiger or leopard.

Upper centre. Elephant crossing the Rapti River.

Lower Centre. Gharial (Gavialis gangeticus) crocodile on the banks of the Narayani river. (Photo: Tiger Tops)

Top right. Sambar deer in open grassland. This deer is one of the prey species of the tiger. (Photo: Tiger Tops)

Lower right. The one-horned rhinoceros (Rhinoceros unicornis). (Photo: Tiger Tops)

Lower Valleys

Trekking begins, in most instances, with either a flight or a bus ride to the point where the walk starts. What could be more impressive than to arrive at Pokhara Airport to be greeted by this incredible view, *upper left*, of the Annapurna Peaks. Often it is a bus ride that gets you to your take-off destination, *lower left*, this one on the road to Trisuli Bazaar and the Langtang Valley. The walk begins. U*pper right* is the town of Gorkha at the start of a trek up the Marsyandi Valley and *lower right* is Henja, at the start of the trail north of Pokhara.

Probably the first contact with the local people will be with the children of the town or village where the walk begins. "Namaste", is the universal greeting *right* and it is also a thank you and a blessing.

The differing character of villages is very often the result of
their location. At *left*, the thatched roofs of a low altitude
village beside the Yangdi Khola north of Pokhara, contrasts
dramatically with the village of Naudanda, *above*, on the
ridge above. Naudanda, with its roofs generally of slate,
has the added advantage of a superb backdrop of the
Annapurna peaks.

These beautifully painted and thatched "round" houses, *above*, near Pamdur, west of Pokhara, each have a small shrine indicated by a sprig of bamboo. Colourful and friendly are just two of the words which may describe the people who live in this area, *centre*. Colourful also is bougainvillea growing on the walls of Gorkha Castle above the town of Gorkha, *right*.

Trekkers, porters and local residents all use the same trails to get from one place to another. These trails may pass through a rice paddy, *left*, or a spectacular gorge like this one on the Marsyandi River, *centre*, or as for this father and son carrying their heavy earthenware pots, *right*, be just a hot dusty path.

As you walk up fertile valleys like this, *above*, the Myagdi Khola, you constantly meet with friendly local families, *centre left*, and adorable children, *right*. The craftwork of the people is always functional, whether it be a fishing net or basket as behind the man, *centre right*, or the beautifully woven mats beneath and being made by the man, *far right*.

36

Some villages, *left*, rarely see the sun because of their location deep within a gorge, while others have enough sun to warm their animals on cold winter days, *upper centre*. Dry stone walls, like these in a village west of the Kali Gandaki, *right*, are common throughout Nepal but are very susceptible to damage by cattle and people. It is not unusual to find "crown of thorns", Euphorbia species, *lower centre*, planted on them for protection.

Maize, along with rice, wheat, barley and millet, is one of the main grain crops grown throughout Nepal. Drying and storage are carried out in many different ways. *Left*, we see cobs drying under the eaves of a house while, *centre*, another method uses poles and a thatched "roof". *Far right*, is a good example of little space being wasted. Here the crop is still awaiting harvest.

It is uncommon to see whole hillsides left uncultivated as here at the confluence of the Trisuli River and the Salankhu Khola, *left*. Only a short distance away terraces are everywhere, *centre*. These are pictured in early spring, and the contrast in late summer, *right*, after the monsoon rains have done their work is marked.

43

In late summer the rice paddies are lush and green, *upper left*, but in winter the terraces are bare and fodder for the animals has to be brought in from elsewhere, *centre*. No trek, of the organised type that is, is possible without the aid of porters, *top right* and *lower right*, who carry very heavy loads over sometimes extremely rough terrain.

As roads are pushed further into the hills, trucks and cars become more common, and the use of pack-trains of donkeys, goats or horses, *left*, decreases. However, almost impenetrable gorges and the high cost of road construction in such terrain may mean they never disappear completely.

Rivers, *centre*, the valleys they form, *right*, and the trails along them are the arteries of travel, communication, trade and sustenance, once the roads are left behind.

Trails serve the same purposes wherever they are found. On the *left*, a group of trekkers are on the move up the Marsyandi near Dharapani while, *upper centre*, goats are being moved down the Trisuli valley above Betrawati. *Below centre*, porters and local people on the trail between Namdu and Kabre on the walk into the Khumbu. There is usually time for pictures of local people, *right*, but care must be taken not to offend, if the subject is unwilling.

There are many things to observe as you move along. Architecture and landscape, *centre*, or what is being dried beside the path, *left*, in this case chillies. The people and their environment are inseparable and with the right approach they are a constant joy. A proud grandmother, *right*, shows off her grandchild.

An early start, *left*, is imperative, especially if photography
is your forté, as the early morning light is invariably best.
Here the trek group is passing a "people place", a rest area
and shade for travellers. They are found along all the
major trails and can be usually recognised by the block for
resting loads and the shelter tree which is an essential part
of the construction. The mountains are always present to
add scale and majesty. This peak, *right*, is Machapuchare,
(6993 m) part of the Annapurna massif north of Pokhara.

The Middle Valleys

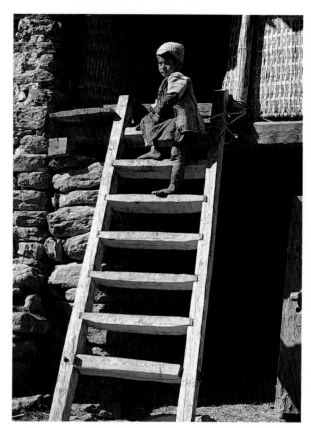

"The wilderness not only encircles us; this prehistoric landscape also prevails within campsites and along the route, which enfolds as we go along."

Reinhold Messner

A young boy climbs a ladder to gain access to the first floor living area of his home (*above*).

As you gain altitude thatched roofs give way to slates or shingles held down with rocks. The mountains are ever present. This scene *left,* is at the top of a small pass above Ghandrung in the Annapurna area north of Pokhara.

Totally different types of landscape can occur at the same altitude. The trail, *left*, perches high above a valley in open country. At *top centre*, a trail at the same altitude leads you through a dense tropical forest. Even the forest type can be different as, *lower left*, we see a temperate forest of conifers and rhododendrons. In spring, if you are lucky, you may be fortunate enough to find one of these lovely orchids, *far right*, Coelogyme ochracea growing on rocks.

Terraces are everywhere. Terraces, *upper left*, are ploughed while further tillage is undertaken by women. Winter is a time of lower activity with bare terraces, *lower left*, but is not always a barren time as these terraces near Tarkum, *centre*, show with the mustard crop beginning to flower.

There is always interest for local people when trekkers are about, especially in the less frequently visited areas. This hillman, crouched amongst the stubble of last summer's crop, found plenty to interest him.

The brown grass of winter, *below*, near Kirantichap contrasts vividly with the lush green of the post monsoon season photographed near Gorkha, *centre*..

The Gurja Himal make an impressive backdrop to Tarkum, *upper right*, while the Ganesh Himal, *lower right*, do the same in this picture of a farm house in the Trisuli valley.

Smoke filters through the roof of this house near Kusum Drangra in the Dudh Khosi valley, *above*. Masons split stone, *right*, for an extension to a school in the Myagdi Khola valley.

A woman, *left*, displays quiet concentration on her sewing and old men enjoy the winter sun. The man, *centre*, was photographed in the upper Kali Gandaki area whereas the man on the *right* lives in Babbychaur to the west.

Travelling across the grain of the country the views from ridges into the valleys below are awesome, as *left*, on the descent to Beni in the Kali Gandaki valley and at *lower left*, on the same descent but at a lower level. Note the erosion-fed alluvial fan in the distance which is forcing the river to change its course.

Crossing a tributary of the Modi Khola, *upper right*. The Langtang Khola above Forest Camp, *centre*. I waited for the sun to rise on this scene and the gradual transformation was magical. River detail of Langtang Khola, *above*.

When trekking it is rewarding to look behind you as well as ahead, for the scene is constantly changing. This picture, *far left*, was taken north-west of Pokhara. Grains form the staple diet of Nepal's population and agriculture is the backbone of its economy. Agriculture is by western standards primitive and lack of fertiliser and an adequate roading system have been continuing handicaps. The Nepali government is, within its means, trying to rectify these problems. Two women, *upper centre*, spin wool while their grain dries in the sun. Grains of different kinds spread to dry at Lukla, *lower centre*. This primitive method of pounding grain, *above*, is common throughout Nepal. Wastage can be a major problem as can getting it dry before the onset of the monsoon in late spring.

Trekking through spring fields near Syabru in the Langtang valley area.

Tatopani suspension bridge over the Kali Gandaki River.   Nilgiri (south peak) is the backdrop.

This colourful sky, *above*, was photographed near Syabru in winter. Bamboo, *right upper*, is found at all altitudes in Nepal up to 3600m and is used for a variety of domestic purposes. Nepal has over 350 species of the Gramineae (grass family). The vermilion bracts of Poinsettia (introduced from Central America), *lower right*, are a common sight in Nepal.

Coniferous forests also have a large altitude range. Here we see "Pinus excelsa", *mid upper right*, against a background of terraced fields in the Trisuli Valley. Rhododendrons, R. arboreum, *far right* and R. barbatum, *mid lower right*, appear throughout Nepal, and are especially beautiful in spring (April to May). These were found in the Langtang Valley in April.

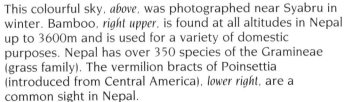

Since trekking began teahouses have sprung up on all popular routes. This one, *above*, has a superb setting deep in the Langtang Gorge north of Kathmandu. *Centre*, a Chetri woman rests from working in the fields close to her home.

Like a patchwork quilt these fields, *right*, straddle the main trail, on a river terrace, in the Kali Gandaki Valley. The crop is mustard grown for its seed which is crushed for oil.

Two family groups that show the distinctive features of races of Tibetan origin, in this case probably Thakalis. The *upper* group live in the Langtang Valley and the *lower* group, who are separating corn, were photographed just below Chame in the Marsyandi Valley.

Thakalis, because of their strategic position on the trade routes between India and Tibet, would regularly traverse this spectacular section of track in the Kali Gandaki Gorge, *above*, and probably built this exposed residence, *right centre*, above Marpha. F*ar right*, smoke rises above Chame in the early morning sunshine.

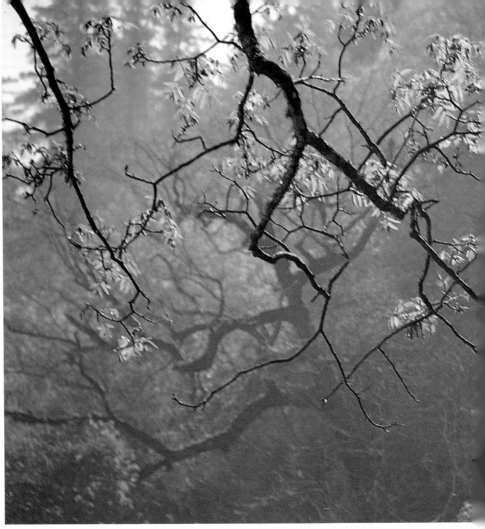

Upper left, R. arboreum near Ghora Tabela. R. arboreum varies from deep red to white and all shades in between. Close-ups, *lower left* and *lower centre*, show pink and white forms. New leaves on deciduous trees are dramatic at this time of year and can be almost as colourful as flowers, as the two *upper centre* illustrations show. The promise of things to come, *far right*, an Ariseama sp. rises through the leaf litter.

Within a few days it is possible to travel from summer to autumn simply by gaining altitude. *Upper left*, shows the colours of autumn in the Upper Marsyandi Khola. The forest floor in winter near Puiyan above the Dudh Khosi, *bottom left*. Sherpas preparing a meal, *centre*, over open fires, the smoke from which strongly resembles a storm moving up the upper Modi Khola Valley, *right*, just below the Annapurna Sanctuary.

The result of the storm on page 79...a snowy breakfast and a fire for warmth, *left*. Storms like this can catch the unaware ill prepared and often result in a dramatic temperature drop, in this case 8 – 10°C in 30 minutes.

Winter, although not a popular trekking time has many rewards for those who go prepared. Snow fall in the Dudh Khosi, *centre*, and cloud give an ethereal touch to trees and prayer flags *above*. Winter is also the time of clear, crisp days with superb mountain views.

Under snow the village, *left*, takes on a sombre mood, but then the sun breaks through, *upper centre*, and the landscape takes on a new perspective. Snow-covered Tukche village, from the south *lower centre*, greets us and before long the mule trains begin to move again, passing through the Chorten-like gate on the northern side of Tukche, *right*.

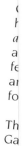

Above is the great Tantric divinity Mahakala, the Great Black One, a Buddhist adoption of a form of the Hindu Bhairab. This one is found in Braga Gompa. *Right* is a gilded relief from the Thyangboche Gompa and, *right centre*, in the same gompa are the drums used by the lamas (monks) in the prayer chamber.

Above is the great Tantric divinity Mahakala, the Great Black One, a Buddhist adoption of a form of the Hindu Bhairab. This one is found in Braga Gompa. *Right* is a gilded relief from the Thyangboche Gompa and, *right centre*, in the same gompa are the drums used by the lamas (monks) in the prayer chamber.

Another feature of entering the high valleys is the appearance of mani walls and stones and many prayer flags, signs of the Buddhist faith. Some mani stones are of considerable size, this one, *above*, is in the Kali Gandaki area. Prayer flags, *right*, fly on houses, passes, monasteries and prominent peaks. On them are printed prayers such as "Om mani padme hum", which when translated means, "Hail to the Jewel of the Lotus", the basic Buddhist chant. This also is the prayer carved into the mani stones.

OṀ MAṆI PADME
HŪṀ
THE PATH OF THE GREAT MANTRA

Carving mani stones, *upper*, gains the carver great merit as it does for the person who commissioned the work and placed it in the wall, *lower*. Mani walls are found all over Nepal, especially in the high valleys or predominantly Buddhist inhabited areas. Custom dictates that travellers pass these walls and stones on the left hand side. Trekkers should follow this custom as a mark of respect to their hosts.

Above is the great Tantric divinity Mahakala, the Great Black One, a Buddhist adoption of a form of the Hindu Bhairab. This one is found in Braga Gompa. *Right* is a gilded relief from the Thyangboche Gompa and, *right centre*, in the same gompa are the drums used by the lamas (monks) in the prayer chamber.

Buddhist monasteries (gompas) have a constant fascination for the visitor and most are accessible to people prepared to follow a few basic conditions. The items they contain, although priceless, are often poorly lit and a torch and flash unit are essential to fully appreciate these treasures. Often it is not until your film is developed that you really appreciate the beauty of some items. In the pictures on these pages I have tried to show the widely contrasting moods to be found as well as the everyday and the unexpected.

This picture, *upper left*, was a surprise — in a small room atop a gompa I was shown these ancient swords and rifles which appeared to be a revered relic of some past event. Whereas elsewhere in the gompa, *lower left*, a more peaceful row upon row of Buddhas and a very prominent Thang-ka. Thang-ka are paintings on cloth of sacred and ceremonial subjects which in Nepal date back to the ninth century. *Above* is the scalp and skeletal hand of a Yeti (abominable snowman) to be found in the Pangboche Gompa in the Khumbu region. The legend lives on . . .

Wall paintings in many gompas are superb. This one, *left*, is from Tragsindo Gompa on the walk into the Solu Khumbu. A pair of ceremonial horns, *right*, from Thyangboche Gompa which was recently severely damaged by fire.

Each gompa has its collection of Buddhas, sacred books, manuscripts and Thang-ka as seen here at Braga Gompa, *upper left*, at Sagar Gompa, *lower left*, and at Tragsindo Gompa, *above*.

Prayer flags silhouetted against Kwangdi Ri lead us to look at some of the higher places, *above*, as do the mani walls, *right*, of the upper Langtang Valley.

Kagbeni is just about as far north as trekkers are allowed to venture in Nepal. To the north lies Mustang, at the time of writing, forbidden territory. Kagbeni, *left*, is an ancient town and is the centre of much that is of interest to geologists as in this area are found the ammonite fossils called "shaligrams" which date back to the early Mesozoic age some 200 million years ago. As with just about anywhere in the world the children of Kagbeni, *above*, are irrepressible.

Namche Bazaar, a prosperous market town,
above, and site of the Sagarmatha National Park
Headquarters, is built in a valley dominated by
mountains. Here we see Kwangdi Ri (6187m).
The town consists of very well constructed
houses, *centre left* and *centre right*, and is, along
with the towns of Khunde and Khumjung,
generally the focal point of the Sherpa inhabited
Khumbu region.

Sherpas *above* and *left*, (from the Tibetan Shar-pa, which means "People from the east") and their close relatives elsewhere in Nepal are of Mongolian extraction. They arrived in Nepal about the 12th century or later, after fleeing from eastern Tibet's Kham region.

Sherpa houses, like these at Pangboche *above*, have a distinctive style of architecture consisting of a single unit with two storeys. The ground floor is for storage and a byre for cattle while upstairs are the family living quarters. The yak *upper right* provides the Sherpa family with many of its requirements. Because of the altitude of Sherpa villages wood for burning is increasingly scarce. Therefore, as in many other high areas of the world, dung is dried for use as a fuel source *lower right*. The use of open fires is traditional in Sherpa homes and the effect of this can be seen in this early morning photograph of Khumjung *far right*.

The architectural style of houses in the upper Marsyandi Valley (near Pisang *upper left*), has one noticeable difference from the houses of the Khumbu area. It is the use of large open terraces facing the sun and used, among other things, for drying grains, wood and skins. Walls of stone slabs and colourful wooden windows are a feature in this area. Wood, because of its close proximity, plays a much greater part, *lower left*, than in the Khumbu.

Siting for the sun is extremely important in the high areas. Windows, doors, byres and terraces are almost always orientated with the sun in mind. This is evident in the two *central* pictures showing a woman spinning in the shelter of a doorway *left* and an old man in front of his house. A good Sirdar (head Sherpa) will always try to site a campsite which gives the best orientation for sun and of course view. This campsite *above* is in front of Braga in the Upper Marsyandi.

The landscape of Nepal is "big", the scale given by the figures in the picture *upper left* is important. No less important to scale are the airstrip and track in this view *centre* of the Marsyandi Valley below Braga. Scale is a relative thing, it is very easy to overlook the world at your feet and tiny gems like this colourful primula *right*. Early morning and a group of Sherpanis (Sherpa women) give scale and depth to this view, *far right* of Nilgiri and part of the Annapurna massif.

Snow is always a possibility at high altitudes and adds another dimension visually, as well as physically. It does that in this view *above* of the Khumbu Valley just below Pheriche and to this scene *upper centre* at Muktinath in the upper Kali Gandaki Valley.

Yaks returning down valley *lower left* after completing a carry to Everest Basecamp, with the peak of Lobuche in the background. Chortens near Muktinath *above right* make a fascinating foreground to this view of Dhaulagiri and Tukche viewed from the north. Ama Dablam (6856m) and a chorten near Pangboche *lower right*.

After the snow comes the melt and another magical time. Here we see snow receding in the superb landscape *left* of the upper Kali Gandaki above Kagbeni. Winter can be a rewarding time to trek as long as you are properly equipped against the cold at high altitudes. The intensity of this is illustrated by this frozen stream *centre*, in the Annapurna Sanctuary, with the south face of Annapurna I (8091m) in the background. A fleeting glimpse *upper right* of East Glacier above Kyanjin Gompa in the Langtang, while down valley spring is making its presence known with the arrival of this beautiful, almost stemless iris (Iris kemaonensis) *left*.

The mountains of Nepal have a constant fascination to climbers and trekkers alike. F*ar left* Makalu (8470m) peeps out from behind closer but no less spectacular peaks in this view up the Imja Khola from a ridge on Taweche in the Khumbu area. L*eft upper* the East Glacier and the interesting striations in the rocks are featured in this telephoto picture.

The effort of walking at high levels cannot be overstated. Even fit people must take things slowly as seen here *above* Duglha in the Khumbu Valley. Overnight dustings of snow are common at high levels whatever the season, this *lower left* was near Tilicho Pass in the Annapurna area.

Ama Dablam (6856m) rises majestically above the Imja Khola *far left* and looks equally impressive from further north near Pheriche *upper left*. Late afternoon offers the chance of additional colour at sunset as seen here *lower left* on Langtang Lirung (7246m) on the walk into the Langtang Valley. Sunshine does not necessarily mean warmth. This picture *above* of the upper Khumbu Valley looking towards Everest Basecamp was taken in sub zero temperatures but does not give that appearance. Pumori (7145m) is the peak on the left.

Early morning view of "the grand barrier" above Tilicho Lake *upper left*, a great view from your tent opening. Annapurna I just peeps over the ridge in the centre. A walk above the Kyanjin Gompa, in the Langtang Valley, to Yala Ri offers excellent views of many peaks and glaciers *lower left*. Early morning in the lower Imja Khola and Mt Everest (Chomolungma to the Sherpa people, Sagarmatha to the Nepalese) just shows above the Nuptse – Lhotse ridge, *far left*.

Once into the high country of Nepal unexpected and spectacular views of high peaks present themselves at almost any time. Walking up the Dudh Kosi, above Lukla, a side valley suddenly opens up an unhindered view, *left*, of Kusum Kangguru (6369m). The same thing happens in the Kali Gandaki, part of the Nilgiri group, *upper centre*, was photographed at sunset. While camped above the Kali Gandaki, waiting for a chance to visit the Dhaulagiri Icefall, the opportunity came *lower centre* to photograph this unusual effect of sunrise on Dhaulagiri (8172m) itself. Traversing the country to the south of the Annapurna Himal, above Dhampus on the Yamdi Khola north of Pokhara, the mountains are always close. Here, *right*, the last rays of the sun catch part of Annapurna II (7937m).

Moving in an easterly or westerly direction in Nepal means a constant series of valleys and ridges due to the drainage system running north-south. It is from these ridge tops that some of the finest views of the Himalaya can be seen. *Above* is the view from the Deorali Pass (3000m) northwest of Pokhara looking east. At *right*, Annapurna South (7256m) and Huinchuli (6435m) tower above the village of Ghandrung.

The Kathmandu Valley

No book on Nepal would be complete without reference to its capital city Kathmandu (population in excess of 300,000). A few scenes are included to whet the appetite rather than satisfy it. The Kathmandu Valley, *above*, has for centuries had an attraction for invaders. This constant succession of rulers has resulted in a city of great cultural, religious and architectural diversity. The pictures which follow highlight that diversity. A view, *far left*, of the valley from the great hill of Swayambhunath in late summer, contrasts with a street scene, *mid left upper*, near the Durbar Square. Rani Pokhari (a shrine surrounded by a manmade lake) was first built in the 16th Century in memory of a son of Pratap Malla. This late afternoon view, *lower left middle*, also shows the clock tower of Tichandra College. Street vendors are everywhere. *Mid upper right* is the colourful display of a jewellery vendor close to Pashupatinath and *lower right centre* a stall in Bhaktapur (Bhadgaon).

People are friendly and a constant fascination to western visitors. This family group *above* was found in Bhaktapur.

The architecture of Kathmandu is unique for its intricate carving, in wood and stone, and its regular use of the pagoda style of construction in many of its buildings. Bhaktapur and Patan (two of the ancient cities which make up Kathmandu) provide many architectural highlights. The superb Sun Dhoka (Golden Gate) which is visible, *upper left*, when you first enter the Durbar Square, Bhaktapur, with *right* a detail of the craftsmanship found above the lintel. This gate was erected in 1753 by Jaya Ranjit Malla.

The Durbar Square in Patan is also a delight. A*bove* is a general view of this square looking north. Immediately to the right of this view of the square is Sundari Chowk, in the centre of which is Tusha Hiti, the sunken royal bath carved from stone in 1670, a small part of which is shown *top right* . Above the sunken bath are a number of superbly carved ornate windows, *centre* . The pagoda style of architecture in Nepal is typified by the Nyatapola Temple, *lower right*, which was built in 1702 by the Malla King, Bupathindra, and can be found just east of the Durbar Square in Bhaktapur.

Buddhism and Hinduism have a remarkably close association in Kathmandu, illustrated in the pictures that follow. *Above* the stupa of Swayambhunath atop its hill which dominates the Kathmandu Valley. This ancient site, thought to date back more than 2500 years, has shrines for both faiths. A feature is the large dorje, *upper right*, or vajra.

During the Bada Dasain festival in September-October each year many blood sacrifices, mainly goat or fowl, are made to the goddess Durga Bhavani. This one, *left*, was made near Bodhnath. This elderly couple, *below*, near Pashupatinath enjoy the warm sun and an inner peace.

On the banks of the Bagmati River is situated one of the most revered Hindu temples in the world, Pashupatinath Temple, which is dedicated to the Lord Shiva. *Lower left* the faithful bathe in the holy water, while just downstream are the funeral ghats which complete the function of Lord Shiva as the "Creator" and the "Destroyer". The Krishna Mandir Temple, *above*, in the Durbar Square in Patan was built around 1637 by King Siddhi Narasingh Malla and is made entirely in stone. Carvings on its friezes depict ancient Hindu epics.

"There is one thing I know, when the mountains
call me, I will always return until I am no more."
Russell Lamb 1982

IN MEMORY OF

Gyaljen Sherpa (*Junbesi*)

Ang Kami (*Khumjung*)

Namgyal (*Namche Bazaar*)

Ang Chering (*Pangboche*)

"The Four Sherpa Trust"

The Four Sherpa Trust was formed in 1985 following the death in an avalanche of four Sherpas who were accompanying a trek in the Tilicho Lake area, Annapurna region, by members of the New Plymouth Tramping (backpacking) Club, New Zealand.

On October 9, 1985, a trekking party of eleven New Zealanders, two Spaniards, nine Sherpas and 22 porters were caught in unseasonal and continuing heavy snowstorms between Tilicho and Meso Kanto Passes at 5482m (16,500 ft). One of the New Zealanders began to suffer symptoms of cerebral oedema (altitude sickness) and in trying to force a route out over the Meso Kanto to Jomoson to get help, four Sherpas were carried away by an avalanche.

With the weather improvement on October 13, two members of the trekking party and a Sherpa set off back to Manang village wearing snowshoes made from the cane seats of trekking stools. They reached Manang three days later and reported the accident to the Himalayan Rescue Association doctor stationed there.

Food was severely rationed and almost exhausted when helicopter contact with the stranded party was finally made on the morning of October 20.

On their return home the New Zealanders set up the Four Sherpa Trust to honour the memory of the dead Sherpas. The Trust's first project was to raise money to fund a radio system, to be run by the Himalayan Rescue Association volunteers, in appreciation for their assistance to the stranded party. Radios were installed, in 1987, in the H.R.A. aid stations at Manang (in the Annapurna area) and Pheriche (in the Everest area). They operate in conjunction with the National Park Service radio network.

The entire proceeds from the sale of this book will be used to maintain these radios, to assist families of Sherpas killed or injured while climbing or trekking, and to help educate their children.

For further information contact: **THE FOUR SHERPA TRUST**, P.O. Box 92, *New Plymouth, New Zealand.*

REFERENCE MATERIAL
GUIDE BOOKS
NEPAL an Insight Guide (Apa Productions)
KATHMANDU and the Kingdom of Nepal by Prakash
A. Raj (Lonely Planet)
A GUIDE TO TREKKING IN NEPAL by Stephen Bezruchka
(The Mountaineers)
TREKKING IN THE NEPAL HIMALAYA by Stan Armington
(Lonely Planet)
KATHMANDU VALLEY by Robert & Linda Flemming
(Allied Publishers Pvt Ltd)
THE HIMALAYAS by Takehide Kazami (Kodansha
International Ltd)
SAGARMATHA, MOTHER OF THE UNIVERSE – THE
STORY OF MT. EVEREST NATIONAL PARK by Margaret
Jefferies (The Mountaineers)
COLLINS GUIDE TO MOUNTAINS AND
MOUNTAINEERING by John Cleare (Collins)

REFERENCE BOOKS
INDIAN WILDLIFE (INCLUDING SRI LANKA & NEPAL) an
Insight Guide (Apa Productions)
FLOWERS OF THE HIMALAYA (2 Vols) by Oleg Polunin
and Adam Stainton (Oxford)
BIRDS OF NEPAL by Robert L. Fleming Sr, Robert L.
Fleming Jr and Lain Singh Bangdel (Fleming)
NEPAL – NATURES PARADISE edited by Trilok Chandra
Majupuria (White Lotus Co. Ltd)
THE ART OF NEPAL by Lydia Aran (Sahayogi Prakashan)
SHERPA ARCHITECTURE by Valerio Sestini and Enzo
Somigli (Unesco)
MONUMENTS OF THE KATHMANDU VALLEY by John
Sanday (Unesco)

OTHER MATERIAL
VIGNETTES OF NEPAL by Harka Gurung (Sajha Prakashan)
H.M.G. OF NEPAL publish a wide variety of guides
designed for visitors.

MAPS
NELLES VERLAG   NEPAL at 1:500,000/1:1,500,000 (includes KATHMANDU
                     VALLEY and KATHMANDU CITY)

NEPAL – Kartenwerk der Arbeitsgemeinschaft fur
vergleichende Hochgebirgsforschung

                     HELAMBU-LANGTANG (N°8) 1:100,000
                     KATHMANDU VALLEY (N°1) 1:50,000
                     LAPCHI KANG (N°3) 1:50,000
                     ROLWALING HIMAL (N°4) 1:50,000
                     TAMBA KOSI (N°6) 1:50,000
                     KHUMBU HIMAL (N°2) 1:50,000
                     EVEREST 1:25,000
                     SHORONG/HINKU (N°5) 1:50,000
                     DUDH KOSI (N°7) 1:50,000

Commissioner: Nelles Verlag,
              Schleissheimer Str. 371,
              D-8000 Munchen 45,
              Telex 5218169
              The Federal Republic of Germany.

Acknowledgements
*Projects, such as the production of this book,
rely on the help and assistance of many people
and organisations. The Trust gratefully
acknowledges the contribution of the following:*

*Michael Radich, of Michael Radich Wine
Merchant, Stratford, New Zealand, distributor
of fine New Zealand wines, for sponsorship of
this publication.*
*Len and Inge Cobb, of Leonard Cobb
Directions, without whose enthusiasm and
drive this book would be but a dream.*
*Warwick Deacock and his company,
Ausventure, of Sydney, Australia, for his
direct assistance and encouragement.*
*Tiger Tops/Mountain Travel International
Group, who operate under the registered trade
mark of Tiger Mountain, for their willingness
to allow the use of images from their photo
library and for the generous assistance in other
areas.*
*Jimmy Roberts of Pokhara, Nepal for his
interest and co-operation in allowing the Trust
the use of original material on the origins of
trekking and adventure travel.*
*The Taranaki Savings Bank for their
generous donation via the Community Grants
Scheme.*
*Snow Lion Publications for the use of their
superb line drawings.*
*Sir Edmund Hillary for his support
and advice.*
*Last, but not least, to my wife, Joan, for her
encouragement and support during this
protracted but fascinating exercise.*

Distributed throughout New Zealand, by
Paul Wadsworth of Wadsworth Books
City Centre, New Plymouth.

Designed by, Leonard Cobb, Auckland,
New Zealand
Finished art, Inge Cobb
Typeset, Ay & Jay Typesetters Ltd,
Auckland
Printing Co-ordination: Leonard Cobb